Dr José van den Akker

The Space Between

THE ART OF CONNECTION ACROSS CULTURES

Copyright © 2026 by Dr José van den Akker (PhD, MEdSt, AdvDipTAT)

All rights reserved. Apart from fair dealing for the purposes of study, research, criticism or review as permitted under the Copyright Act, no part of this publication may be reproduced, distributed or transmitted in any form or by any means without prior written permission.

Cover design by Judith San Nicolas
Typeset in Nunito 12 pt, Arial Nova 14 pt, Great Vibes 28 pt
Printed and bound in Australia by IngramSpark
Prepared for publication by Dr Juliette Lachemeier @ The Erudite Pen

A catalogue record for this book is available from the National Library of Australia

The Space Between: The Art of Connection Across Cultures

ISBN 9781764422901
eISBN 9781764422918

Every time two people from different worlds meet, a bridge is built, or a wall. Cross-cultural work is about learning how to build that bridge with care. It's about remembering that real dialogue isn't just speaking—it's listening deeply enough to be changed by what you hear.

Dr José van den Akker (PhD, MEdSt, AdvDipTAT)

Contents

PREFACE 1

1. THE CALL TO CROSS.................................7
- The Inner Cross..8
- A Poem for the Turning..9
- The World Between Worlds.......................................11
- From Anxiety to Wonder...12
- The Practice of Crossing..13

2. THE SHELL..15
- The Contact Boundary..16
- When Boundaries Harden..17
- The Field Between..18
- The Practice of Softening...19
- Stories in the Bark..20
- Becoming Permeable...21

3. FIXED ATTENTION 23
- The Lens of Either/Or..24
- The Space Between..25
- An Encounter in the room...25
- The Addiction to Fixing..27
- The Art of Unfixing..27
- From Duality to Dialogue...28
- A Practice of Attention...29
- Becoming Whole..30

4. HOLDING THE SPACE 33

Creating Safe Ground for Dialogue and
Transformation 33
The Ground Beneath Us 34
How to Hold Space 35
The Circle of Trust 36
The Teacher as Witness 37
The Quiet Courage 38
Silence as a Teacher 39
Creating Communitas 39
The Gift of Presence 40

5. THE CROSSROADS OF TRANSFORMATION 43

Standing at the Cross 44
Listening becomes Learning 45
The Alchemy of Not-Knowing 46
Meeting the Shadow 47
From Fragment to Flow 47
Practices for Crossing 48
Living the Both/And 49
The Gift of Transformation 50

6. THE SPACE BETWEEN WORLDS 51

Living Connection in Everyday Life 51
The Invisible Threads 52
Ordinary Crossings 53
Living the Field 54
Embodied Dialogue 55
Art as a Bridge 56
Living as Dialogue 57

    A Practice of Presence.. 57
    Weaving It All Together 58
    The Everyday Invitation... 59

7. REWEAVING THE WEB................................. 61

    A Culture of Connection and Compassion............ 61
    From Systems to Stories... 62
    The Education of the Whole Being 63
    Leadership as Stewardship... 64
    Communities as Living Systems............................... 65
    The Practice of Compassion 66
    Small Acts, Wide Ripples.. 67
    A Culture of Connection... 67
    Becoming the Web... 68

8. BECOMING WHOLE 71

    The Invitation to Remember 71
    The Whole That Holds Us 73
    Listening as a Way of Life... 73
    The Gentle Work... 74
    An Invitation.. 74
    A Blessing for the Crossing 75

AFTERWORD: A LIVING PRACTICE 77

GLOSSARY 79

ACKNOWLEDGMENTS 91

Preface

This book began as a doctoral journey—a deep inquiry into how people from different worlds meet, misunderstand, and transform one another. Originally written as a PhD thesis on cross-cultural dynamics, it sought to understand how dialogue, awareness, and creativity could bridge cultural divides. But as the years unfolded, I came to realise that what I was really studying was the human heart: its fragility, its resilience, and its endless longing to connect.

The academic language that once framed my research could not hold the fullness of that discovery. What was needed was a story—a way to speak not only to the mind but to the spirit. This book is that story. It is both reflection and invitation: a call to live with openness, curiosity, and compassion in a world that too often forgets how interconnected it truly is.

Every encounter between people from different worlds offers a chance to remember who we are. Some meetings are soft, full of curiosity. Others sting or confuse us. Yet each one holds an invitation: to pause, to breathe, and to see what happens when "I" and "You" begin to listen.

This book grew from many years of teaching, travelling and wondering—years spent in classrooms, deserts, different organisations, and the quiet space of reflection where culture meets consciousness. Originally it was a PhD study about *cross-cultural dynamics*. But as the research unfolded, I realised that the deeper story was not about systems or theories. It was about people—their hearts, fears, hopes, and the mysterious energy that connects us all.

I also realised that 'culture' has nothing to do with countries or races. Every group of people has its own culture; a groupmind.

Academic language could not hold that story. It needed a human voice.

What follows is not a manual or a theory, but a journey. It explores what happens when we dare to look beyond the surface of difference; when we stop trying to fix or control and instead begin to notice the delicate threads that weave us together.

It is a call to slow down, to feel, and to let new ways of knowing emerge.

1. The Call to Cross

"Your beliefs are maps you lay over the world—and then you see only what the map allows."

—Karl Weick

Every culture, every groupmind offers its own map of reality: how to behave, what to value, what to fear

When our maps collide, we feel disoriented. We may defend, argue, withdraw, or try to convert the other. Yet this friction—the crossing itself—is where growth begins.

For years I taught *Expression and Communication* to groups of people from many different backgrounds. We spoke different languages, carried different stories, and held different ideas about what it meant to communicate. I noticed that beneath our words ran a deeper conversation—a silent current of emotion, energy and expectation. Sometimes it flowed easily. Sometimes it became entangled. The more I paid attention, the more I saw that our struggles in the room mirrored the world outside: the global classroom of humanity still learning how to live together.

Modern education often treats people as if they were machines—collections of neurons, minds to be filled, problems to be fixed. In that model, creativity and intuition become "extras." But when we reduce life to mechanics, we forget the soul that moves within it. Moreover, soul forms the communication. Reducing life to mechanics, we lose the space where real dialogue happens.

I began to wonder: what if education, and life itself, are not about *filling* but about *remembering*? What if cross-cultural work is less about managing difference and more about awakening connection?

2. Listening Across the Divide

Imagine two people standing at opposite sides of a river. Each calls out, but the wind bends their words.

To hear one another, they must stop shouting and begin to listen—not just with the ears but with the whole body.

That is the art of crossing worlds.

Listening in this way asks for stillness. It asks us to suspend judgment long enough for something new to appear between us. Physicist David Bohm called this the *implicate order*; the hidden wholeness in which everything participates. When we listen with the heart, we begin to sense that order. We glimpse the world not as separate parts, but as a living conversation.

In my teaching and research, I saw that misunderstanding was rarely caused by ignorance alone. More often it came from *fixed attention*—the mind's habit of clinging to certainty. When attention softens, awareness widens, and we can finally meet one another in the living present.

3. The Invitation

This book is an invitation to explore that space—the thin, shimmering line between self and other. Through stories, reflections, and simple practices, we will look at how culture and each groupmind shapes perception, how belief becomes identity, and how awareness can transform conflict into creativity.

You will not find neat answers here. Instead, you will find openings: doorways into your own experience. The purpose is not to change who you are, but to help you *remember* that who you are already includes the other. Let us begin where all true dialogue begins—with attention, curiosity, and the willingness to be changed

1. The Call to Cross

Every time we meet another human being, we cross an invisible threshold. We step out of the familiar world of our own assumptions and into the shimmering space of uncertainty—a space where something new can happen.

At first, that space can feel uncomfortable. We may feel anxious, unsure, even defensive. Yet that tension is sacred. It is the heat in which new understanding is forged. Without friction we cannot walk.

When I began teaching *Expression and Communication*, I saw these crossings every day. Students from different cultural backgrounds came together in one room, each carrying a private landscape of memories and meanings. Some brought enthusiasm, others suspicion. A few had learned to speak softly so as not to offend; others spoke loudly to make sure they were heard.

In those moments, I realised that education is not just about sharing knowledge. It is about learning how to *be* with one another—how to hold the space between differences without rushing to fill it with explanations or corrections.

True communication, I discovered, begins not with speaking but with *presence*.

The Inner Cross

The word *cross* is heavy with history. In many traditions it stands for suffering, division, or sacrifice. But it also carries another meaning—transformation.

To "cross" is to move from one state of being to another. It is the moment when two directions meet, forming a point of choice.

Every cross-cultural meeting holds such a point.

The Call to Cross

Do we stay within the comfort of our familiar beliefs, or do we risk crossing into unknown territory? When we choose to cross, something inside us begins to shift.

The boundary between "self" and "other" softens. We realise that difference is not the enemy of unity; it is the doorway to it.

A Poem for the Turning

warped

as the sun sets

and we walk our paths

too few of us in reverence

enriching life

but caught up in having to have or be

disappointment about

our common loss

too few of us allot

to hold infringement of space

crowding space instead

carmachines and cultured lands

roads that normalise our paths

as Knowledge becomes extinct

chasing money, status and wins

rather than balanced living

whilst educating children

to keep up the crazy pace

if they snub, we drug

how much deeper can

fallen angels fall?

how much mercy

can us be granted?

I cry deeply within

lament collective spirit

as too few of us give it life

I long for the desert

where I can sing her songs

and maintain the space

but destined I am to be here

where few can hear my call

if only they'd listen

if only I could

and enunciate the wind.

This poem came to me during a period of exhaustion and longing—the kind of weariness that comes from witnessing a world that seems to have lost its rhythm. It was a prayer to remember what really matters: the quiet pulse of life beneath all our striving.

Poetry can do what theory cannot. It bypasses the intellect and speaks directly to the heart. It helps us feel the *cross* within ourselves—the tension between our higher knowing and our habitual rushing, between wisdom and the noise of the everyday.

The World Between Worlds

In every culture I've encountered, I see the same hunger: a desire to belong, to be seen, to contribute something meaningful. Yet our systems—especially in education—often trap that desire inside narrow definitions of success. We teach competition instead of cooperation, performance instead of presence.

Cross-cultural education, at its best, is an act of remembering. It reminds us that learning does not belong to institutions. It is the birthright of every human being who has the courage to stay curious.

The moment we stop trying to fix, label or defend, we begin to listen differently. We hear the subtle voices that live beneath words—the rhythm of breathing, the vibration of feeling, the music of silence.

That is where true dialogue begins.

From Anxiety to Wonder

Anxiety is often seen as a problem to be solved. But in cross-cultural encounters, it can be a guide. It tells us that something precious is at stake: our sense of identity, belonging, or truth.

When we treat anxiety as information rather than failure, it becomes a teacher. It asks us: *What am I clinging to? What am I afraid to see?* Answering those questions gently, without blame, is how transformation begins.

The space between cultures or groups can feel like a wound. But it can also be a womb—the birthplace of new ways of seeing. If we learn to stay with discomfort long enough, it reveals its wisdom.

The Practice of Crossing

Everyday life offers endless chances to practice this art.

When you feel misunderstood, pause. Notice your breath.

Feel the boundary of your own "shell"—what in Dutch I call *schil*, the thin membrane between self and other.

Inside that contact boundary lives both your vulnerability and your strength.

If you listen carefully, you may sense how porous it really is—how your emotions, thoughts, and energy are always in quiet conversation with those around you. You can sense the conversation, but it does not need to overwhelm you.

Crossing worlds is not about giving up who we are. It is about becoming more whole by recognising the other as part of ourselves.

Dr José van den Akker

This is the work of our time: to rediscover connection in an age of separation. To move from information to wisdom, from reaction to awareness, from control to compassion.

And it begins, always, with attention.

(✦)

In the next chapter, we'll explore *The Shell*: how the invisible boundaries we carry shape our encounters—and how we can learn to soften them without losing ourselves.

2. The Shell

Every being carries an invisible shell. It is the fine boundary where we touch the world—the place where "I" ends and "You" begins, though the edge is never as clear as it seems.

In Dutch, the word is *schil*: the skin, the bark, the husk that holds life and yet allows it to breathe. Without a shell we would dissolve; with one that is too hard, we cannot feel. Cross-cultural work begins here—in learning how to soften the shell without breaking it.

Dr José van den Akker

The Contact Boundary

Think of a snail.

It moves slowly, aware of every vibration through the ground. When danger comes, it withdraws into its shell—not out of weakness, but for protection. We humans do the same. Our shell is made of habits, language, memories, and beliefs.

Each culture teaches its children what to keep inside and what to show the world. We learn how loud to laugh, when to look away, how to greet, how to disagree. These gestures become part of our shell—a map of safety and belonging.

But when two shells meet, something interesting happens.

If both are too rigid, they simply collide. If both are too open, they may merge and lose shape. The art of communication lies in finding the *flexible edge*—that living membrane where exchange becomes possible.

Psychology calls this the *contact boundary*. In that thin space, energy flows in both directions.

It is where learning, healing and relationship take place.

And, like any living surface, it can be bruised or numbed. When cultures meet after histories of pain or domination, their shells remember.

When Boundaries Harden

In one of my teaching experiences, two students—one from an Aboriginal Australian community, the other from a European background—were assigned to work together. They sat side by side yet remained oceans apart. Each was polite, cautious, uncertain how to reach across the invisible line.

During a drawing exercise, the Aboriginal student sketched a series of concentric circles connected by lines—a traditional symbol of people gathering. Her partner looked puzzled and said, "I don't understand this kind of art." The first student hesitated, then replied quietly, "That's okay. It's not meant to be understood. It's meant to be felt."

In that moment, I saw both shells harden—one with confusion, the other with retreat. Neither student was wrong; both were protecting something precious. But understanding could only arise if they dared to stay at that trembling edge of not-knowing.

Rigid boundaries feel safe but they isolate. Porous boundaries feel risky but they allow life to move.

Crossing worlds requires the courage to keep the edge alive.

The Field Between

Imagine every conversation as a small ecosystem. The thoughts, gestures, silences and feelings between us form an invisible field—a shared atmosphere.

When that field is open, ideas flow like wind through trees. When it is closed, the air grows heavy.

Modern science calls such patterns *complex dynamics*. They show us that everything—people, cultures, even systems—interacts like weather: sensitive, unpredictable, alive. A single kind word can shift the whole climate of a room. A careless remark can freeze it.

The Shell

When we learn to sense the field between us, we start to understand communication not as transmission but as *relationship*. We realise that meaning is co-created, not delivered.

This awareness asks us to slow down. To notice not only what is said, but what *wants* to be said. Not only what we know, but what we feel beneath the knowing.

The Practice of Softening

You can explore your own shell through simple reflection:

1. **Pause before responding.**

    Notice the micro-moment when you tense or prepare your defence. That is your shell tightening.

2. **Breathe into the edge.**

    Let the breath remind your body that safety is already here. You do not have to close off.

3. **Listen for resonance.**

    Instead of asking "Do I agree?", ask "What part of me recognises this?"

4. **Speak from the heart.**

    Words that come from presence, not persuasion, soften the field.

With practice, this becomes an art—the art of remaining open while staying whole.

Stories in the Bark

In every forest, the bark of a tree carries its history: fire scars, wind cracks, initials carved by human hands.

Our shells too bear the marks of what we have survived. They are not signs of failure but of life.

When we meet others, we meet their bark as well as their being. To truly see another person is to sense the forest behind them—the storms they have weathered, the light they have sought.

Cross-cultural understanding grows when we honour these layers instead of rushing past them. We learn to ask, *what story does this pattern protect?* And, *what new growth might emerge if the shell were gently touched, not broken?*

Becoming Permeable

As we soften, something unexpected happens: we begin to feel the larger rhythm that holds us all. Boundaries blur into belonging. The "I" becomes part of a wider "We."

This is not the loss of identity but its expansion. Like skin that breathes, we learn to inhale the world and exhale ourselves into it.

The shell remains—but now it glows from within.

(✦)

In the next chapter, we'll explore *Fixed Attention*: how our mind's habit of control keeps us trapped in duality, and how simple awareness can free us to experience the world as an unfolding conversation rather than a set of rules.

3. Fixed Attention

We live in a world that worships certainty.

We are trained from childhood to sort life into neat boxes: right and wrong, good and bad, success and failure, self and other.

This habit of division feels natural because it gives us the illusion of control. But when we look closer, we see that reality itself refuses to stay in its boxes.

The truth, like water, keeps slipping through.

Dr José van den Akker

The Lens of Either/Or

In every culture there are invisible lenses through which people see. These lenses are shaped by history, religion, language, and fear.

They filter our vision until we no longer see what *is*, only what fits our idea of how things should be.

When I worked in cross-cultural contexts, I often saw this lens in action. A teacher might say, "My students either understand or they don't."

A student might think, "I either belong here or I don't."

An institution might believe, "We're either successful or we've failed."

Such thinking flattens the rich texture of human experience into a binary code—zero or one, yes or no.

It mirrors the logic of machines, not of living systems.

In reality, growth is messy. Understanding flickers on and off like a candle in wind.

Belonging is a rhythm, not a rule.

The Space Between

The mind loves clarity, but life moves in paradox. Between night and day lies twilight.

Between joy and sorrow lies tenderness. Between cultures lies the trembling space where learning truly begins.

When we cling to either/or, we miss that middle space—the living conversation between opposites.

We harden our shells, defend our position, and lose touch with the subtle intelligence that connects all things.

Complexity theory reminds us that life evolves not through certainty but through tension—the creative friction between order and chaos. In that sense, confusion is not the enemy of understanding; it is its birthplace.

An Encounter in the room

I once asked a group of adults from various backgrounds to draw how they saw "communication." Some drew speech bubbles or telephones. Someone sketched two trees with roots intertwined underground.

When she explained that "real communication happens beneath words," the group fell silent. Then a young man from Australia frowned and said, "But if we don't say what we mean, how will people know?"

Both were right—and both were limited by their cultural habits of meaning.

In that moment, we could have chosen sides: who's right, who's wrong. We could have had 'sticking sides'.

Instead, I asked them to imagine communication as *music*: sound and silence, each defining the other.

As we discussed, I saw eyes soften, laughter return. Something invisible had shifted.

We were no longer trying to prove who was correct. We were listening for harmony.

The Addiction to Fixing

In modern education and politics alike, the drive to "fix" things has become a kind of addiction. We try to fix people, systems, even emotions. But fixing often means freezing—holding something still so that we don't have to feel its movement.

When we say "this is the way it is," we shut down the possibility of change.

When we say "it must be one or the other," we forget that life includes both.

In truth, most things are not problems to be solved but relationships to be tended.

The Art of Unfixing

To unfix attention is to loosen the grip of control. It does not mean drifting aimlessly; it means seeing freshly.

You can practice this in small, ordinary ways:

- When you feel certain, pause and ask, *what else might be true?*

- When you feel judged, ask, *what might the other person be protecting?*
- When you feel stuck, move your body—walk, breathe, look at the sky. The body knows how to shift attention when the mind cannot.

Each time you do this, you re-enter the space of dialogue.

You step out of the narrow hallway of either/or and into the spacious room of both/and.

From Duality to Dialogue

The philosopher David Bohm once said that the word "dialogue" means "flow of meaning."

It is not a debate or negotiation; it is a current that moves between people and transforms them both.

Fixed Attention

To live dialogically is to stop trying to win or lose. It is to notice the energy that connects us even when we disagree.

It is to trust that truth is not a possession but a meeting place.

When we enter dialogue with life itself—with our students, our neighbours, our own inner voices—we begin to see the dance of opposites as creative, not conflicting.

Masculine and feminine, reason and intuition, science and spirituality—these are not enemies. They are partners in evolution.

A Practice of Attention

Try this small meditation:

1. Sit quietly and recall a recent disagreement or tension.
2. Instead of replaying who was right, sense what each side was protecting.

3. Feel the energy that lies *between* those sides—the pulse of life trying to express itself.
4. Breathe into that pulse. Let it soften your sense of separation.

In that breath, you may glimpse what physicist David Bohm called "the implicate order"—the invisible wholeness from which all opposites arise. It is not something to understand but something to feel.

Becoming Whole

The world does not need more people who are certain; it needs more people who can hold uncertainty with grace. To work across cultures, across beliefs, even across our own inner divides, is to practice wholeness—to remember that we are not fragments but reflections of a single unfolding story.

Wholeness does not erase difference; it honours it. It says: *Both can be true.* It says: *There is room for all of us at the table.*

Fixed Attention

When we learn to rest our attention in that larger field, compassion becomes natural.

We no longer defend the self against the other, because we see that the self is made of the other. We become, simply, human.

$$(\ast)$$

In the next chapter, we will explore *Holding the Space*: how to create environments—in classrooms, communities, and within ourselves—where transformation can unfold safely and authentically.

4. Holding the Space

Creating Safe Ground for Dialogue and Transformation

Real transformation does not happen through persuasion.

It happens when we feel safe enough to stop defending and start listening.

In every classroom, family, or meeting room, there comes a moment when words no longer work. The air thickens; eyes turn away; hearts retreat behind polite silence. That is the moment we need to *hold the space*.

To hold space is to stay present when others cannot.

It is to make room for what is real, even when it is messy.

It is to trust that something deeper than logic is trying to come through.

The Ground Beneath Us

In my years of working and teaching across cultures, I came to see that the most powerful learning did not happen when I was explaining—it happened when I was listening deeply.

Students learned best when they sensed that the room itself was kind.

Kindness is not sentimentality. It is a form of steadiness—a quality of attention that says, *You are safe here. You can unfold at your own pace.*

When we create such a field, people begin to relax the armour they wear.

Defences soften, stories emerge, and healing begins almost by itself.

This is not only emotional safety. It is *ontological* safety—the feeling that it is safe to exist, to be seen, to take up space as you are.

Without this, no amount of theory can reach the soul.

How to Hold Space

Holding space is less about technique and more about presence.

Yet presence can be cultivated.

Here are some guiding attitudes:

1. **Begin with humility.**

    You don't have to know the answer. Begin instead with the question: *What wants to be heard right now?*

2. **Listen with your whole body.**

    Notice tone, posture, silence. Meaning often hides between words.

3. **Pause before you respond.**

   A moment of stillness allows emotion to settle and truth to surface.

4. **Protect the edges.**

   Ensure everyone in the group has voice and respect. Boundaries are not walls; they are containers for trust.

5. **Stay curious.**

   Curiosity is the opposite of fear. It turns confrontation into discovery.

When these qualities are present, space itself becomes the teacher.

The Circle of Trust

In a workshop, I invited participants to sit in a circle, each sharing a story about a communication experience that mattered – positive or difficult.

At first, people communicated cautiously, testing whether the group would judge them.

But as listening deepened, using art making as a tool to self-reflect, so did honesty.

One woman spoke of being treated as 'special' in her community, leaving her feeling left out. Another admitted that she feared saying the wrong thing and being called racist.

By the end of the workshop, the tension in the group had melted into tenderness.

No one had fixed anything, yet something invisible had healed.

We had discovered that inclusion is not achieved through slogans but through shared vulnerability.

This is the essence of holding space: creating a climate where truth can breathe.

The Teacher as Witness

In traditional education, the teacher is expected to lead, to know, to control. But in transformative education, the teacher becomes a witness—one who stands beside rather than above.

Witnessing is an act of respect. It says, *I see you. I will not rush to interpret your story through my lens.*

This shift from control to companionship changes everything. The classroom becomes a living organism, self-organising, responsive.

Learning becomes mutual—a dance rather than a delivery.

The Quiet Courage

Holding space demands courage—not the loud, heroic kind, but the quiet courage of staying open when it would be easier to close.

It asks us to resist the impulse to rescue others from their discomfort.

Discomfort is part of growth. Our task is not to remove it but to tend it—to hold it with compassion until it reveals its teaching.

In cross-cultural contexts, this often means staying present with pain that is not ours: the pain of history, injustice, loss.

To hold space for such pain is sacred work. It turns empathy into practice.

Silence as a Teacher

Silence can feel awkward in cultures addicted to speed and speech. Yet in silence, we begin to hear the subtle layers beneath conversation: the unspoken grief, the yearning for belonging, the wisdom that words cannot carry.

In Indigenous traditions around the world, silence is not emptiness but listening.

It is a way of honouring the spirit that moves through all things.

When we allow silence in our teaching, therapy, or daily life, we offer people the dignity of their own timing.

Transformation happens in its own rhythm, not ours.

Creating Communitas

Anthropologist Victor Turner used the word *communitas* to describe the deep sense of unity that can arise among people who share a threshold experience—a time of transition, vulnerability, and mutual recognition.

When we hold space well, communitas appears almost naturally. It is not planned or produced; it is felt—like warmth spreading through a room.

In that moment, we remember what it means to be human together. Differences don't vanish, but they stop dividing.

We realise that each of us is a mirror, reflecting a part of the whole.

The Gift of Presence

To hold space is to offer presence as a gift. It is to become a still point in the turning world—a reminder that peace is not found elsewhere, but here, in awareness itself.

We do not need to fix the world before we can love it.
We need only be willing to *stay with it*—to sit quietly beside what hurts until it begins to soften in our shared gaze.

This is how dialogue becomes healing, and how education becomes an act of love.

(✦)

In the next chapter, we'll explore *The Crossroads of Transformation*: what happens when holding space leads us into the unknown—the threshold between endings and beginnings, chaos and creation.

5. The Crossroads of Transformation

Living the Both/And

Every genuine encounter brings us, sooner or later, to a crossroads.

One road leads back to the familiar—the safety of what we already know.

The other leads into uncertainty—the open field where growth happens.

At this threshold, we often feel torn. Part of us longs to leap forward; another part wants to turn back.

The mind demands clarity; the soul asks for surrender.

This is the sacred tension of transformation—the place where endings and beginnings meet.

Standing at the Cross

The symbol of the cross has followed humanity for millennia.

Long before it was religious, it was cosmic: the meeting of vertical and horizontal, heaven and earth, spirit and matter.

To stand at that intersection is to feel the pull of opposites within ourselves—the longing to transcend and the need to belong.

In cross-cultural work, we meet this cross every day.

When two worldviews collide, something must die—an assumption, a certainty, a small piece of ego. If we can stay with the discomfort long enough, that dying makes space for something larger to be born.

Transformation, then, is not a leap into perfection but a slow unlearning of our defences.

It is the art of standing in contradiction without collapsing into despair.

Listening becomes Learning

When we walk on country, listen with your feet.

You can't rush the land. You wait until it speaks to you, with you at the centre.

This carries a way of being—patient, relational, embodied.

For many participants from Western backgrounds, this way of knowing feels both alien and deeply familiar, as if an ancient muscle is remembering how to move.

It is a practice of listening, not only to ourselves and others in conversations, but to the silence between sentences.

Something invisible will shift—a new field will form.

That field *is* the crossroads: where intellect meets intuition, where listening becomes learning.

The Alchemy of Not-Knowing

Modern culture trains us to fear not-knowing.

We equate uncertainty with failure. Yet every creative act begins with a pause, a gap, an emptiness.

The potter cannot shape the clay without space in the centre of the bowl.

The musician cannot make music without silence between the notes.

In the same way, transformation requires an emptying—a willingness to let go of what we think we know.

When we stop grasping for answers, awareness itself begins to reorganise us.

This is the quiet alchemy of the crossroads: the moment when surrender becomes strength.

Meeting the Shadow

Crossing into the unknown also means meeting what we have avoided—our shadow.

The shadow is not evil; it is the part of us that has been denied love.

In cross-cultural encounters, shadow often appears as projection: the traits we dislike in others are mirrors of what we fear in ourselves.

To meet the shadow with compassion is to reclaim lost energy.

It is to see that every culture, like every person, carries both light and darkness.

Acknowledging this frees us from moral superiority and invites mutual humility.

Only then can dialogue become genuine healing.

From Fragment to Flow

In physics, there is a point where solid turns to liquid—when heat melts rigidity into movement.

The same happens in human systems.

When awareness warms the frozen structures of fear, life begins to flow again.

This flow is the hallmark of transformation.

It is unpredictable, relational, alive.

It doesn't ask for control, only participation.

At the crossroads, we discover that being human is not a problem to solve but a rhythm to join.

Practices for Crossing

1. **Breathe with the paradox.**

    When opposites pull you apart, inhale both sides. Let the breath remind you they share the same air.

2. **Name the threshold.**

    Whisper to yourself, *something is ending, something is beginning.* Naming honours the transition.

3. **Create ritual.**

    Light a candle, walk in nature, paint,

dance—give the invisible a form your body can understand.

4. **Trust the pause.**

   Growth often hides in stillness. Let silence do its quiet work.

Living the Both/And

Maturity is not choosing sides but learning to hold them.

We are both fragile and resilient, individual and collective, rooted and free.

When we stop fighting these truths, we discover a deeper harmony—the music of wholeness.

To live the both/and is to walk through life as a bridge.

Sometimes that means being misunderstood by both shores.

But bridges are not built for comfort; they are built for connection.

Dr José van den Akker

The Gift of Transformation

Transformation is not an event but a way of being.

It begins wherever we are willing to stay awake.

It asks us to meet difference without fear and change without resistance.

Every time we do, the world becomes a little more whole.

And perhaps that is the quiet purpose of all cross-cultural work—not to erase boundaries, but to illuminate the sacred space between them.

(✦)

In the next chapter, we'll explore *The Space Between Worlds*: how to live with openness once we have crossed—integrating the lessons of difference into daily life, relationships, and creative practice.

(✦)

6. The Space Between Worlds

Living Connection in Everyday Life

After every crossing comes the question: *How do we live now?*

How do we bring the openness of transformation back into the noise and rhythm of daily life—the emails, the traffic, the misunderstandings, the thousand small crossings that make up a day?

Transformation may begin in silence or insight, but its truth is tested in relationship.

The challenge is not only to awaken, but to *stay awake while shopping for groceries, while teaching a class, while disagreeing kindly with someone you love.*

This is where practice becomes life.

The Invisible Threads

Every meeting leaves a trace—a subtle imprint of energy, emotion, and meaning.

We often think we act as isolated individuals, but beneath the surface we are woven into a living fabric of connection.

In Indigenous Australian thinking, this fabric might be called *Country*: a field of relationship that includes land, ancestors, plants, animals, and people.

In systems theory, it is the *field*—the emergent whole that shapes and is shaped by each part.

In spiritual traditions, it is the *web of life*.

Different names, same truth: nothing exists alone.

Once we sense this, our awareness begins to change.

A conversation is no longer just words between two people; it is a ripple through the fabric of being.

A choice made in fear tightens the weave; a choice made in compassion loosens it.

We begin to realise that our smallest gestures—a glance, a tone of voice, a pause—participate in the evolution of the whole.

Ordinary Crossings

One afternoon, while queuing at a café, I watched a young woman struggle with her phone. She looked flustered, apologising to the barista for taking so long. The barista smiled and said gently,

"It's okay—everyone forgets sometimes."

The tension dissolved. The woman laughed; her shoulders dropped. Something beautiful passed between them—not dramatic, but unmistakable.

It was the simplest form of cross-cultural healing: two strangers meeting in their shared humanity.

Moments like this remind us that transformation is not limited to workshops or retreats. It happens in the grocery store, at traffic lights, in the way we hold the gaze of someone who feels unseen.

The sacred is woven through the ordinary.

Living the Field

When we truly recognise connection, responsibility changes shape.

It is no longer a burden of obligation but a form of care.

We start to sense when the field around us is tense or open, heavy or light, and we can respond with awareness.

If the space feels closed, we might soften our tone.

If the space feels frantic, we might slow our breathing.

If the space feels fragmented, we might share a story that restores coherence.

In this way, we become co-creators of the collective field.

The work of cross-cultural understanding becomes less about fixing difference and more about tending to the energy that moves between us.

Embodied Dialogue

To live connection is to include the body.

The body is the meeting place of worlds—biological, emotional, cultural, spiritual.

When we ignore it, we lose our compass.

Next time you feel misunderstood or reactive, notice what your body does.

Does it tighten, shrink, rush?

Can you stay with that sensation without judging it?

That awareness itself begins to shift the field.

The body does not lie. It speaks the language of truth long before words arrive.

When we listen to its signals, dialogue deepens—not only between people, but within ourselves.

Art as a Bridge

Art has always known how to speak across boundaries.

A painting, a song, a dance—these bypass the intellect and go straight to the heart, where understanding lives before language.

In art therapy sessions, I have seen people from vastly different backgrounds find connection without a single shared word.

Colour, shape, and rhythm became their common tongue.

Art invites us to play in the space between worlds.

It reminds us that creation and communication are the same act—both require presence, both reveal the unseen.

Living as Dialogue

To live in the space between worlds is to live as dialogue itself —to meet life not as an object to be controlled but as a partner to be listened to.

This way of living asks:

- What is life saying to me right now?
- How might I respond in harmony rather than in haste?
- What wants to unfold through this meeting?

When we begin to ask such questions, our days become conversations with existence.

We move through the world like musicians in a shared improvisation—listening, responding, leaving space for others' notes to shine.

A Practice of Presence

Each morning, before the day begins, take a few moments to notice the field around you.

1. Feel your feet on the ground—the cross between earth and sky and the space around you within your own body.
2. Invite awareness to expand beyond the skin, sensing the room, the trees, the earth deep down beneath you, the distant hum of life.
3. Whisper silently: *I am part of this web.*
4. Throughout the day, return to this knowing whenever you feel separate or afraid.

Presence, once remembered, turns ordinary moments into communion.

Weaving It All Together

We began this journey with difference—the friction and confusion of crossing cultures. We discovered the shell that protects us, the boundaries that shape contact, the stillness that holds dialogue, the paradox that transforms.

Now we see that all these threads are one weaving: the practice of awareness-in-relationship.

To understand others is to understand ourselves. To honour the space between is to honour life itself.

Every time we meet another being with openness, we repair a small tear in the fabric of the world.

The Everyday Invitation

The invitation is simple, but not easy:

Stay awake.

Stay kind.

Stay connected, even when it hurts.

Let every encounter—with friend, stranger, or shadow—remind you that the space between is alive, waiting to teach us how to be human together.

And in that quiet space, if you listen closely, you might hear the whisper that has always been there:

You are part of the whole. You always were.

7. Reweaving the Web

A Culture of Connection and Compassion

When a web is broken, no single thread can repair it.

It takes the whole pattern—each strand, each intersection—coming alive again through attention and care.

The same is true for our human world.

Fragmented by fear, competition, and isolation, we have forgotten how deeply our lives depend on one another.

But beneath the noise, a quiet movement is stirring—people everywhere rediscovering connection, compassion, and community.

To reweave the web is to become part of that movement.

From Systems to Stories

For decades, education and leadership have been shaped by systems that prize efficiency over empathy, and information over imagination and inspiration.

We measure outcomes but rarely ask about meaning.

We train minds but neglect hearts.

We teach communication skills but forget to cultivate listening.

Yet when I look at what truly changes lives, it is not data—it is story.

Stories awaken the part of us that knows we belong. We are weaving and the weavers of a grand narrative.

In every culture, stories were once the way wisdom was passed: through fireside tales, dances, songs, dreams.

When we reintroduce story into our teaching, healing, or leadership, we reawaken the oldest technology of all—human connection.

Try this simple shift: instead of asking, *"What should I teach?"* ask, *"What story wants to be told here?"*

Instead of asking, *"How do I lead?"* ask, *"How do I listen?"*

Stories make systems human again.

The Education of the Whole Being

Education, at its heart, is not the transmission of knowledge but the awakening of consciousness.

It is how a culture teaches its young—and itself—to see.

If we are to reweave the web, we must educate for wholeness: for empathy as much as intellect, for creativity as much as compliance, for awareness as much as achievement.

This means bringing the body, emotion, and spirit back into learning spaces.

It means valuing the quiet student who feels deeply as much as the one who speaks fluently.

It means creating classrooms where curiosity is stronger than fear.

Imagine schools and universities where silence is as honoured as speech, where students learn not only to analyse but to *attune*, where the arts are recognised as languages of knowing.

Such education would not only inform—it would *transform*.

Leadership as Stewardship

Reweaving the web also requires a new kind of leadership—one rooted in presence rather than power.

A true leader is a steward of space. They hold the field in which others can grow. They understand that authority comes not from control but from integrity—from the alignment between inner awareness and outer action.

In a meeting or classroom, such leadership feels like calm clarity.

It doesn't dominate; it invites.

It trusts that wisdom is distributed, not centralised.

When leaders model humility, dialogue becomes natural.

When they practice transparency, trust follows.

When they embody compassion, the culture changes without a slogan.

Communities as Living Systems

A community is not a collection of individuals but a living ecology of relationships.

Each voice, each silence, each gesture contributes to its health.

Like any ecosystem, a community thrives on diversity.

Difference is not disorder; it is the raw material of resilience.

When we fear difference, we create monocultures—fragile systems that collapse under stress.

When we honour difference, we create complexity—systems that adapt, evolve, and flourish.

To reweave the web is to move from *control* to *coherence*: from imposing order to sensing pattern, from managing people to cultivating belonging.

The Practice of Compassion

Compassion is not pity; it is perception. It sees through the illusion of separation and recognises the shared pulse beneath.

To live compassionately is to hold both truth and tenderness.

It is to see injustice clearly without becoming hardened, to face suffering without closing the heart.

Compassion is courage in gentle form.

In cross-cultural work, compassion often begins with humility—the willingness to see how little we know of another's story, and how much our own well-being depends on theirs.

From that humility arises respect. From respect, relationship. From relationship, renewal.

Small Acts, Wide Ripples

The web is reknit through small acts: a conversation held with patience, a child encouraged to express rather than suppress, a leader who chooses honesty over image.

These gestures may seem insignificant, yet they ripple outward.

Each moment of genuine connection strengthens the collective field. Each act of awareness becomes a thread of healing in the larger tapestry of life.

When we remember this, our work—whatever form it takes—becomes sacred service.

A Culture of Connection

A culture of connection is not built overnight. It grows wherever people choose to replace fear with curiosity, judgment with empathy, isolation with participation.

In such a culture:

- Teachers see learners as co-creators.
- Organisations value reflection as much as results.
- Art and science walk hand in hand.
- The invisible—silence, intuition, imagination—is recognised as real.

This is not utopia. It is simply a return to balance, to the wisdom that every living system already carries.

Becoming the Web

At last, we realise that there is no "web" to fix—because *we are the web*.

Every breath, thought, and relationship is a strand in its design.

When we live with that awareness, connection ceases to be a theory; it becomes a way of being.

To reweave the web is to live as love in motion—a quiet, steady practice of remembering that everything belongs.

8. Becoming Whole

The Invitation to Remember

Wholeness is not something we achieve; it is something we remember.

Like a melody we once knew by heart, it waits beneath the noise of striving.

Every act of attention, every moment of compassion, brings us a little closer to that remembering.

Dr José van den Akker

The Long Journey Home

We began this journey with difference—with the confusion, wonder, and challenge of meeting other worlds.

Along the way, we discovered that those crossings were never only about culture; they were about consciousness.

To understand others, we had to listen more deeply to ourselves.

To embrace diversity, we had to embrace our own inner multiplicity.

Each chapter of this journey—the shell, the cross, the tension, the silence, the field—has been a mirror.

Together they form a map, not of escape, but of return.

Home, it turns out, is not a place.

It is a way of seeing—a way of being in which nothing and no one is left outside the circle of care.

The Whole That Holds Us

If we could see through the eyes of wholeness, we would see that everything belongs: the joy and the grief, the knowing and the confusion, the self and the other, the visible and the unseen.

Wholeness is not perfection. It is the acceptance of complexity—the ability to hold light and shadow in the same breath.

It is the moment when we stop dividing life into categories and start dancing with it as it is.

In that dance, paradox becomes rhythm. Difference becomes texture. And love becomes the silent current that carries us all.

Listening as a Way of Life

When awareness becomes listening, life itself becomes dialogue.

Every sound, every encounter, every silence becomes a message.

The wind against the window whispers impermanence.

A child's laughter teaches trust. A stranger's frown invites empathy. Even our own mistakes speak—if we are willing to hear.

To live in this way is to participate consciously in creation.

We are no longer observers of life but collaborators with it.

The Gentle Work

Wholeness asks for gentle courage—not the kind that conquers, but the kind that stays.

It is the courage to stay present when things fall apart, to stay kind when the world feels hard, to stay curious when fear says "enough."

Gentleness is not weakness. It is strength without aggression, clarity without rigidity, love without possession.

It is the quiet revolution that reweaves the web from within.

An Invitation

So I offer this as a simple invitation:

Slow down.

Breathe.

Notice what is moving between you and the world.

When you feel divided, soften your attention.

When you feel lost, listen for what is calling you home.

When you feel small, remember that you are part of a much larger pattern—one that needs your presence exactly as you are.

The space between is not a gap to be crossed; it is a meeting place to be inhabited.

It is where humanity learns to recognise itself.

A Blessing for the Crossing

May you walk gently through difference, finding wisdom in what you do not yet understand.

May your shell stay soft enough to feel and strong enough to protect what is tender.

Dr José van den Akker

May you listen for the quiet rhythms beneath the noise and find beauty in the spaces between words.

May you become the bridge where worlds can meet —not by effort, but by presence.

And may you remember, again and again, that wholeness is not elsewhere.

It is here, waiting in the stillness of your own becoming.

Afterword: A Living Practice

This book began as an academic thesis—a study of *cross-cultural dynamics*.

It ends as an invitation to live those dynamics as daily practice.

Theory has become story.

Analysis has become relationship.

Research has become reverence.

If the journey has touched you, let it continue through you—in your conversations, your teaching, your art, your way of walking in the world.

Because each time you meet another with openness, you are helping to reweave the web of life.

And that—quietly, courageously—is how the world changes.

Glossary

A Note for the Reader

This glossary is intended as a companion to the text, inviting readers to return to concepts not as fixed definitions, but as living references shaped by their own experience.

Some concepts in this book originate from Dutch and cross-cultural pedagogical traditions that do not translate neatly into English. Where this is the case, the original term is retained and gently unfolded through explanation rather than reduced to a single equivalent. These words are offered not as fixed definitions, but as invitations to notice how meaning lives in image, relationship, and experience.

You are encouraged to return to this glossary as a living reference, allowing terms to deepen as your reading — and your own reflections — unfold.

Throughout the glossary, concepts drawn from complexity are intentionally contrasted with reductionist ways of thinking, reflecting the book's commitment to relational, emergent, and lived understanding rather than fixed explanation.

Attention

An active, living quality of awareness rather than a narrow focus on outcomes. Attention, as used in this book, is the capacity to stay present with what is unfolding—internally and relationally—allowing dialogue, insight, and connection to emerge.

Attentive Engagement

A form of mindful participation that notices not only what is happening, but how the mind reacts. Attentive engagement involves staying with sensation, emotion, and meaning without being driven by habit, judgment, or the pursuit of stimulation.

Attractor

A concept from complexity theory describing patterns toward which systems naturally move. In human experience, attractors can be unconscious beliefs, habits of attention, emotional patterns, or relational dynamics that repeatedly shape perception, behaviour, and outcomes — either creatively or restrictively.

See also: Strange Attractor

Autoethnography

A way of knowing (and doing research) that weaves personal experience with cultural and social reflection. In *Crossing Worlds*, lived experience is treated not as anecdotal but as a legitimate source of insight into how meaning, identity, and connection are formed.

Beeldspraak (Image Language)

A Dutch concept referring to communication through images, metaphors, symbols, and embodied expression rather than literal explanation. Beeldspraak speaks directly to lived and felt experience and often reveals meaning that rational language cannot reach. In *Crossing Worlds*, beeldspraak is central to dialogue across cultures, where images can bridge differences that words alone cannot.

(See also: *Oerbeeld*)

Blind Spots

Unseen or unacknowledged patterns that shape perception and behaviour. Blind spots often arise from fear, habit, or fixed attention, and can lead to repetitive misunderstandings in relationships and cross-cultural encounters.

Bricolage

The art of working creatively with what is already present. Bricolage values fragments, contradictions, and partial knowing, allowing meaning to emerge through relationship rather than linear logic. In this book, bricolage reflects the weaving together of story, theory, practice, and lived experience.

Bricoleur

One who practices bricolage. The bricoleur accepts uncertainty and incompleteness, recognising that understanding the human condition is an ongoing, relational process rather than a finished product.

Boxed Realities

Fixed ways of seeing (fixed viewpoints) that isolate people, ideas, or cultures from their wider context. Boxed realities simplify complexity but limit understanding, often reinforcing either/or thinking.

Chiasmus

A figure of crossing, symbolised by the letter X, and in my PhD thesis 'Understanding and Working with the Dynamics in Cross-Cultural Education) referred to as *the Cross* (+). Chiasmus represents moments where opposites meet—self and other, knowing and not-knowing—creating the possibility of transformation rather than closure.

Complexity

The dynamic interaction of many elements that gives rise to patterns greater than the sum of their parts. Human relationships, cultures, and communities are *complex systems*: sensitive, adaptive, and alive.

Complexity recognises that meaning and behaviour emerge through interaction rather than linear cause and effect. Small changes can have wide ripples, and uncertainty is not a flaw but a natural condition of living systems.

See also: Reductionist Thinking

See Chapter 7 · 'Reweaving the Web'

Reductionist Thinking

An approach to understanding that breaks life into isolated parts and treats those parts as if they function independently. Reductionist thinking seeks certainty, prediction, and control, often overlooking context, relationship, and lived experience.

In *Crossing Worlds*, reductionist thinking is contrasted with complexity. Where reductionism simplifies, complexity holds nuance; where reductionism controls, complexity listens; where reductionism seeks fixed answers, complexity stays responsive to what is unfolding.

Reductionist approaches can be useful for technical problems, but when applied to human systems they often lead to fragmentation, misunderstanding, and loss of meaning.

See Chapter 3 · 'Fixed Attention — The Trap of Either/Or Thinking'

Conceived Values

Values adopted through social conditioning rather than lived experience. Conceived values may guide behaviour, but they can also conflict with deeper, organismic knowing.

See Organismic Values

Conceptual Metaphor

A symbolic structure that shapes how we understand experience. In *Crossing Worlds*, metaphors such as the cross, the shell, the field, and the space between help make invisible dynamics tangible and felt.

Contact Boundary

The living edge where self meets other. This boundary is neither rigid nor dissolved; it is a flexible membrane through which relationship, learning, and healing occur.

See Chapter 2 · 'The Shell'

Field

An invisible relational space created between people, cultures, or systems. The field carries emotional tone, meaning, and possibility, and shifts in response to attention, presence, and interaction.

Fixed Attention

The mind's tendency to cling to certainty, control, and familiar interpretations. Fixed attention narrows perception and reinforces dualistic thinking, making genuine dialogue difficult.

See Chapter 3 · 'Fixed Attention — The Trap of Either/Or Thinking'

Groupmind

The shared patterns of belief, emotion, and behaviour that emerge within any group. Groupmind shapes what feels normal, acceptable, or threatening, often operating below conscious awareness.

Holding Space

The practice of staying present, non-defensive, and attentive in moments of uncertainty, discomfort, or vulnerability. Holding space allows truth to emerge without forcing resolution.

See Chapter 4 · 'Holding the Space'

Oerbeeld (Primordial Image)

A foundational inner image that shapes perception, meaning, and orientation in the world. Oerbeelden operate beneath language and cognition, influencing how individuals and cultures experience reality. In *Crossing Worlds*, oerbeelden are understood as deep imaginal structures that silently guide behaviour, belief, and belonging.

(See also: *Beeldspraak*)

Morphic Field

A concept describing collective patterns of memory and form that influence behaviour across time and space. In this book, morphic fields resonate with the idea of the relational field that carries shared history and potential.

Organismic Values

Values that arise from direct, lived experience rather than external authority. Organismic values tend to support vitality, coherence, and authentic relationship.

Shadow

Parts of the self or culture that have been denied, suppressed, or disowned. In cross-cultural encounters, shadow often appears through projection, misunderstanding, or moral superiority.

Shell (Schil)

The protective structure formed by habits, beliefs, language, and cultural norms. The Dutch term *schil* emphasises the shell as a living contact-boundary rather than a barrier. It provides safety and identity, yet must remain flexible for genuine meeting and growth to occur. When the schil becomes rigid, connection hardens; when it softens, dialogue becomes possible.

See Chapter 2 · 'The Shell'

Slipping Communication

Moments when meaning fails to land as intended, often due to fixed viewpoints or unspoken assumptions. Slipping communication reveals the need for slowing down and re-attuning to the relational field.

Strange Attractor

A term from complexity theory describing a dynamic pattern that never exactly repeats yet remains coherent over time. Strange attractors help explain how living systems — including individuals, relationships, and cultures — can appear unpredictable while still following an underlying order.

In *Crossing Worlds*, strange attractors offer a way of understanding recurring relational patterns, cultural tensions, and moments of transformation that do not resolve into stability, but continue to evolve through attention and presence.

See Chapter 7 · 'Reweaving the Web'

The Space Between

The relational, liminal zone where transformation occurs. Neither self nor other, neither certainty nor chaos, the space between is where new understanding can arise.

See Chapter 6 · 'The Space Between Worlds'

Threshold

A moment or space of transition where something is ending and something new is beginning. Thresholds invite presence, humility, and willingness to not yet know.

See Chapter 5 · 'The Crossroads of Transformation'

Wholeness

The capacity to hold complexity without fragmentation. Wholeness does not erase difference; it integrates light and shadow, self and other, into a living sense of belonging.

See Chapter 8 · 'Becoming Whole'

Acknowledgments

My heartfelt gratitude goes to the many people who shared their stories, their courage, and their wisdom along this journey. To my students and colleagues who taught me that learning is a shared act of discovery; to the communities that welcomed me across cultures and landscapes; and to those who inspired me to look deeper when understanding seemed out of reach.

To my family and friends—thank you for your patience, love, and belief in this work. And to the unseen teachers—nature, silence, and time—thank you for reminding me that connection is the essence of life.

About the Author

Dr José van den Akker is a transpersonal art therapist, educator, and researcher with a lifelong interest in the meeting points between culture, consciousness, and creativity. Holding a PhD in Cross-Cultural Education and Communication and an Advanced Diploma in Transpersonal Art Therapy, she integrates art, dialogue, and reflective practice to help people explore their inner and outer worlds. Her work invites individuals and communities to rediscover connection through awareness, imagination, and compassion.

Also by Dr José van den Akker

Universal Heart: Connecting You at the Centre of Your Cross

Understanding and working with the dynamics in cross-cultural education (thesis)

Enjoyed the book?
You can follow Dr José van den Akker at:

Website: www.universal-heart.com.au/

Email: jose@universal-heart.com.au

LinkedIn: www.linkedin.com/in/dr-jose-van-den-akker/

Facebook: www.facebook.com/DrJosevandenAkker/

Instagram: www.instagram.com/drjosevandenakker

www.ingramcontent.com/pod-product-compliance
Lightning Source LLC
LaVergne TN
LVHW051219070526
838200LV00064B/4966